What Teachers Do When No One Is Looking

by Jim Grant and
Irv Richardson

Illustrated by Patrick Belfiori

Published by
Crystal Springs Books • Peterborough, New Hampshire
1-800-321-0401

Published by Crystal Springs Books
10 Sharon Road, PO Box 500
Peterborough, NH 03458
1-800-321-0401
www.crystalsprings.com
www.sde.com

09   08   07   9   10   11   12

ISBN 1-884548-17-2

Art Director and Production Coordinator: Soosen Dunholter
Illustrator: Patrick Belfiori

We dedicate this book to educators who work with other people's children and help all of us by building a better future one life at a time, student by student – even *when no one is looking.*

Teachers teach the 3 R's.

Teachers enjoy
time with their families.

Teachers drive.

Teachers read.

Teachers love yard sales.

Teachers recycle.

Teachers spend money.

Teachers go holiday shopping.

Teachers get fresh air.

Teachers sit.

Teachers try to
shop for groceries.

Teachers work 9:00 to 3:00.

Teachers go to the theatre.

Teachers bake.

Teachers go out at night.

Teachers practice many careers.

Teachers take the summer off.

And while no one is looking
teachers touch lives.